Marilyn

©. ANDRE DE Dienes

09–12.2004

SEPTEMBER	OCTOBER	NOVEMBER	DECEMBER
1 We	1 Fr	**WEEK 45**	1 We
2 Th	2 Sa	1 Mo	2 Th
3 Fr	3 Su	2 Tu	3 Fr
4 Sa	**WEEK 41**	3 We	4 Sa
5 Su	4 Mo	4 Th	5 Su ◗
WEEK 37	5 Tu	5 Fr ◗	**WEEK 50**
6 Mo ◗	6 We ◗	6 Sa	6 Mo
7 Tu	7 Th	7 Su	7 Tu
8 We	8 Fr	**WEEK 46**	8 We
9 Th	9 Sa	8 Mo	9 Th
10 Fr	10 Su	9 Tu	10 Fr
11 Sa	**WEEK 42**	10 We	11 Sa
12 Su	11 Mo	11 Th	12 Su ●
WEEK 38	12 Tu	12 Fr ●	**WEEK 51**
13 Mo	13 We	13 Sa	13 Mo
14 Tu ●	14 Th ●	14 Su	14 Tu
15 We	15 Fr	**WEEK 47**	15 We
16 Th	16 Sa	15 Mo	16 Th
17 Fr	17 Su	16 Tu	17 Fr
18 Sa	**WEEK 43**	17 We	18 Sa ◖
19 Su	18 Mo	18 Th	19 Su
WEEK 39	19 Tu	19 Fr ◖	**WEEK 52**
20 Mo	20 We ◖	20 Sa	20 Mo
21 Tu ◖	21 Th	21 Su	21 Tu
22 We	22 Fr	**WEEK 48**	22 We
23 Th	23 Sa	22 Mo	23 Th
24 Fr	24 Su	23 Tu	24 Fr
25 Sa	**WEEK 44**	24 We	25 Sa
26 Su	25 Mo	25 Th	26 Su ○
WEEK 40	26 Tu	26 Fr ○	**WEEK 53**
27 Mo	27 We	27 Sa	27 Mo
28 Tu ○	28 Th ○	28 Su	28 Tu
29 We	29 Fr	**WEEK 49**	29 We
30 Th	30 Sa	29 Mo	30 Th
	31 Su	30 Tu	31 Fr

01–04.2005

JANUARY

1 Sa
2 Su
WEEK 1
3 Mo ☽
4 Tu
5 We
6 Th
7 Fr
8 Sa
9 Su
WEEK 2
10 Mo ●
11 Tu
12 We
13 Th
14 Fr
15 Sa
16 Su
WEEK 3
17 Mo ☾
18 Tu
19 We
20 Th
21 Fr
22 Sa
23 Su
WEEK 4
24 Mo
25 Tu ○
26 We
27 Th
28 Fr
29 Sa
30 Su
WEEK 5
31 Mo

FEBRUARY

1 Tu
2 We ☽
3 Th
4 Fr
5 Sa
6 Su
WEEK 6
7 Mo
8 Tu ●
9 We
10 Th
11 Fr
12 Sa
13 Su
WEEK 7
14 Mo
15 Tu
16 We ☾
17 Th
18 Fr
19 Sa
20 Su
WEEK 8
21 Mo
22 Tu
23 We
24 Th ○
25 Fr
26 Sa
27 Su
WEEK 9
28 Mo

MARCH

1 Tu
2 We
3 Th ☽
4 Fr
5 Sa
6 Su
WEEK 10
7 Mo
8 Tu
9 We
10 Th ●
11 Fr
12 Sa
13 Su
WEEK 11
14 Mo
15 Tu
16 We
17 Th ☾
18 Fr
19 Sa
20 Su
WEEK 12
21 Mo
22 Tu
23 We
24 Th
25 Fr ○
26 Sa
27 Su
WEEK 13
28 Mo
29 Tu
30 We
31 Th

APRIL

1 Fr
2 Sa ☽
3 Su
WEEK 14
4 Mo
5 Tu
6 We
7 Th
8 Fr ●
9 Sa
10 Su
WEEK 15
11 Mo
12 Tu
13 We
14 Th
15 Fr
16 Sa ☾
17 Su
WEEK 16
18 Mo
19 Tu
20 We
21 Th
22 Fr
23 Sa
24 Su ○
WEEK 17
25 Mo
26 Tu
27 We
28 Th
29 Fr
30 Sa

05–08.2005

MAY

1 Su ◗

WEEK 18

2 Mo
3 Tu
4 We
5 Th
6 Fr
7 Sa
8 Su ●

WEEK 19

9 Mo
10 Tu
11 We
12 Th
13 Fr
14 Sa
15 Su

WEEK 20

16 Mo ◖
17 Tu
18 We
19 Th
20 Fr
21 Sa
22 Su

WEEK 21

23 Mo ○
24 Tu
25 We
26 Th
27 Fr
28 Sa
29 Su

WEEK 22

30 Mo ◗
31 Tu

JUNE

1 We
2 Th
3 Fr
4 Sa
5 Su

WEEK 23

6 Mo ●
7 Tu
8 We
9 Th
10 Fr
11 Sa
12 Su

WEEK 24

13 Mo
14 Tu
15 We ◖
16 Th
17 Fr
18 Sa
19 Su

WEEK 25

20 Mo
21 Tu
22 We ○
23 Th
24 Fr
25 Sa
26 Su

WEEK 26

27 Mo
28 Tu ◗
29 We
30 Th

JULY

1 Fr
2 Sa
3 Su

WEEK 27

4 Mo
5 Tu
6 We ●
7 Th
8 Fr
9 Sa
10 Su

WEEK 28

11 Mo
12 Tu
13 We
14 Th ◖
15 Fr
16 Sa
17 Su

WEEK 29

18 Mo
19 Tu
20 We
21 Th ○
22 Fr
23 Sa
24 Su

WEEK 30

25 Mo
26 Tu
27 We
28 Th ◗
29 Fr
30 Sa
31 Su

AUGUST

WEEK 31

1 Mo
2 Tu
3 We
4 Th
5 Fr ●
6 Sa
7 Su

WEEK 32

8 Mo
9 Tu
10 We
11 Th
12 Fr
13 Sa ◖
14 Su

WEEK 33

15 Mo
16 Tu
17 We
18 Th
19 Fr ○
20 Sa
21 Su

WEEK 34

22 Mo
23 Tu
24 We
25 Th
26 Fr ◗
27 Sa
28 Su

WEEK 35

29 Mo
30 Tu
31 We

09–12.2005

SEPTEMBER	OCTOBER	NOVEMBER	DECEMBER
1 Th	1 Sa	1 Tu	1 Th ●
2 Fr	2 Su	2 We ●	2 Fr
3 Sa ●	**WEEK 40**	3 Th	3 Sa
4 Su	3 Mo ●	4 Fr	4 Su
WEEK 36	4 Tu	5 Sa	**WEEK 49**
5 Mo	5 We	6 Su	5 Mo
6 Tu	6 Th	**WEEK 45**	6 Tu
7 We	7 Fr	7 Mo	7 We
8 Th	8 Sa	8 Tu	8 Th ◖
9 Fr	9 Su	9 We ◖	9 Fr
10 Sa	**WEEK 41**	10 Th	10 Sa
11 Su ◖	10 Mo ◖	11 Fr	11 Su
WEEK 37	11 Tu	12 Sa	**WEEK 50**
12 Mo	12 We	13 Su	12 Mo
13 Tu	13 Th	**WEEK 46**	13 Tu
14 We	14 Fr	14 Mo	14 We
15 Th	15 Sa	15 Tu	15 Th ○
16 Fr	16 Su	16 We ○	16 Fr
17 Sa	**WEEK 42**	17 Th	17 Sa
18 Su ○	17 Mo ○	18 Fr	18 Su
WEEK 38	18 Tu	19 Sa	**WEEK 51**
19 Mo	19 We	20 Su	19 Mo
20 Tu	20 Th	**WEEK 47**	20 Tu
21 We	21 Fr	21 Mo	21 We
22 Th	22 Sa	22 Tu	22 Th
23 Fr	23 Su	23 We ◗	23 Fr ◗
24 Sa	**WEEK 43**	24 Th	24 Sa
25 Su ◗	24 Mo	25 Fr	25 Su
WEEK 39	25 Tu ◗	26 Sa	**WEEK 52**
26 Mo	26 We	27 Su	26 Mo
27 Tu	27 Th	**WEEK 48**	27 Tu
28 We	28 Fr	28 Mo	28 We
29 Th	29 Sa	29 Tu	29 Th
30 Fr	30 Su	30 We	30 Fr
	WEEK 44		31 Sa ●
	31 Mo		

53. WEEK

12.2004 | 01.2005

Monday Montag Lundi Lunes Lunedì Segunda-feira Maandag 月

27

Tuesday Dienstag Mardi Martes Martedì Terça-feira Dinsdag 火

28

Wednesday Mittwoch Mercredi Miércoles Mercoledì Quarta-feira Woensdag 水

29

Thursday Donnerstag Jeudi Jueves Giovedì Quinta-feira Donderdag 木

30

Friday Freitag Vendredi Viernes Venerdì Sexta-feira Vrijdag 金

31

Saturday Samstag Samedi Sábado Sabato Sábado Zaterdag 土

1

New Year's Day | Jour de l'An |
Nouvel An | Neujahr | Capodanno |
Nieuwjaarsdag | Año Nuevo | Ano Novo

Sunday Sonntag Dimanche Domingo Domenica Domingo Zondag 日

2

1. WEEK

01.2005

Monday	3	10	17	24	31
Tuesday	4	11	18	25	1
Wednesday	5	12	19	26	2
Thursday	6	13	20	27	3
Friday	7	14	21	28	4
Saturday	8	15	22	29	5
Sunday	9	16	23	30	6
WEEK	**1**	**2**	**3**	**4**	**5**

Monday Montag Lundi Lunes Lunedì Segunda-feira Maandag 月

(UK) (CDN)
Public Holiday | Jour Férié

3

Tuesday Dienstag Mardi Martes Martedì Terça-feira Dinsdag 火

(UK) Public Holiday (Scotland only)

4

Wednesday Mittwoch Mercredi Miércoles Mercoledì Quarta-feira Woensdag 水

5

Thursday Donnerstag Jeudi Jueves Giovedì Quinta-feira Donderdag 木

(D) Heilige Drei Könige (teilweise)
(A) (E) (I) Heilige Drei Könige |
Reyes | Epifania

6

Friday Freitag Vendredi Viernes Venerdì Sexta-feira Vrijdag 金

7

Saturday Samstag Samedi Sábado Sabato Sábado Zaterdag 土

8

Sunday Sonntag Dimanche Domingo Domenica Domingo Zondag 日

9

2. WEEK

01.2005

Monday Montag Lundi Lunes Lunedì Segunda-feira Maandag 月

●   (J) Coming-of-Age Day

10

Tuesday Dienstag Mardi Martes Martedì Terça-feira Dinsdag 火

11

Wednesday Mittwoch Mercredi Miércoles Mercoledì Quarta-feira Woensdag 水

12

Thursday Donnerstag Jeudi Jueves Giovedì Quinta-feira Donderdag 木

13

Friday Freitag Vendredi Viernes Venerdì Sexta-feira Vrijdag 金

14

Saturday Samstag Samedi Sábado Sabato Sábado Zaterdag 土

15

Sunday Sonntag Dimanche Domingo Domenica Domingo Zondag 日

16

3. WEEK

01.2005

Monday	17	24	31	7	14
Tuesday	18	25	1	8	15
Wednesday	19	26	2	9	16
Thursday	20	27	3	10	17
Friday	21	28	4	11	18
Saturday	22	29	5	12	19
Sunday	23	30	6	13	20
WEEK	3	4	5	6	7

Monday Montag Lundi Lunes Lunedì Segunda-feira Maandag 月

(USA) Martin Luther King Day

17

Tuesday Dienstag Mardi Martes Martedì Terça-feira Dinsdag 火

18

Wednesday Mittwoch Mercredi Miércoles Mercoledì Quarta-feira Woensdag 水

19

Thursday Donnerstag Jeudi Jueves Giovedì Quinta-feira Donderdag 木

20

Friday Freitag Vendredi Viernes Venerdì Sexta-feira Vrijdag 金

21

Saturday Samstag Samedi Sábado Sabato Sábado Zaterdag 土

22

Sunday Sonntag Dimanche Domingo Domenica Domingo Zondag 日

23

4. WEEK

01.2005

Monday	24	31	7	14	21
Tuesday	25	1	8	15	22
Wednesday	26	2	9	16	23
Thursday	27	3	10	17	24
Friday	28	4	11	18	25
Saturday	29	5	12	19	26
Sunday	30	6	13	20	27
WEEK	**4**	**5**	**6**	**7**	**8**

Monday Montag Lundi Lunes Lunedì Segunda-feira Maandag 月

24

Tuesday Dienstag Mardi Martes Martedì Terça-feira Dinsdag 火

○   Ⓘ Tu B'Shevat

25

Wednesday Mittwoch Mercredi Miércoles Mercoledì Quarta-feira Woensdag 水

26

Thursday Donnerstag Jeudi Jueves Giovedì Quinta-feira Donderdag 木

27

Friday Freitag Vendredi Viernes Venerdì Sexta-feira Vrijdag 金

28

Saturday Samstag Samedi Sábado Sabato Sábado Zaterdag 土

29

Sunday Sonntag Dimanche Domingo Domenica Domingo Zondag 日

30

5. WEEK

01|02.2005

Monday Montag Lundi Lunes Lunedì Segunda-feira Maandag 月

31

Tuesday Dienstag Mardi Martes Martedì Terça-feira Dinsdag 火

1

Wednesday Mittwoch Mercredi Miércoles Mercoledì Quarta-feira Woensdag 水

2

Thursday Donnerstag Jeudi Jueves Giovedì Quinta-feira Donderdag 木

3

Friday Freitag Vendredi Viernes Venerdì Sexta-feira Vrijdag 金

4

Saturday Samstag Samedi Sábado Sabato Sábado Zaterdag 土

5

Sunday Sonntag Dimanche Domingo Domenica Domingo Zondag 日

6

6. ■ WEEK

02.2005

Monday	7	14	21	28	7
Tuesday	8	15	22	1	8
Wednesday	9	16	23	2	9
Thursday	10	17	24	3	10
Friday	11	18	25	4	11
Saturday	12	19	26	5	12
Sunday	13	20	27	6	13
WEEK	6	7	8	9	10

Monday Montag Lundi Lunes Lunedì Segunda-feira Maandag 月

7

Tuesday Dienstag Mardi Martes Martedì Terça-feira Dinsdag 火

●

8

Wednesday Mittwoch Mercredi Miércoles Mercoledì Quarta-feira Woensdag 水

9

Thursday Donnerstag Jeudi Jueves Giovedì Quinta-feira Donderdag 木

10

Friday Freitag Vendredi Viernes Venerdì Sexta-feira Vrijdag 金

(J) Commemoration of the Founding
of the Nation

11

Saturday Samstag Samedi Sábado Sabato Sábado Zaterdag 土

12

Sunday Sonntag Dimanche Domingo Domenica Domingo Zondag 日

13

7. ∎ WEEK

02.2005

Monday Montag Lundi Lunes Lunedì Segunda-feira Maandag 月

14

Tuesday Dienstag Mardi Martes Martedì Terça-feira Dinsdag 火

15

Wednesday Mittwoch Mercredi Miércoles Mercoledì Quarta-feira Woensdag 水

16

Thursday Donnerstag Jeudi Jueves Giovedì Quinta-feira Donderdag 木

17

Friday Freitag Vendredi Viernes Venerdì Sexta-feira Vrijdag 金

18

Saturday Samstag Samedi Sábado Sabato Sábado Zaterdag 土

19

Sunday Sonntag Dimanche Domingo Domenica Domingo Zondag 日

20

8. WEEK

02.2005

Monday	21	28	7	14	21
Tuesday	22	1	8	15	22
Wednesday	23	2	9	16	23
Thursday	24	3	10	17	24
Friday	25	4	11	18	25
Saturday	26	5	12	19	26
Sunday	27	6	13	20	27
WEEK	**8**	**9**	**10**	**11**	**12**

Monday Montag Lundi Lunes Lunedì Segunda-feira Maandag 月

(USA) President's Day

21

Tuesday Dienstag Mardi Martes Martedì Terça-feira Dinsdag 火

22

Wednesday Mittwoch Mercredi Miércoles Mercoledì Quarta-feira Woensdag 水

23

Thursday Donnerstag Jeudi Jueves Giovedì Quinta-feira Donderdag 木

○

24

Friday Freitag Vendredi Viernes Venerdì Sexta-feira Vrijdag 金

25

Saturday Samstag Samedi Sábado Sabato Sábado Zaterdag 土

26

Sunday Sonntag Dimanche Domingo Domenica Domingo Zondag 日

27

9. ∎ WEEK

02|03.2005

Monday	28	7	14	21	28
Tuesday	1	8	15	22	29
Wednesday	2	9	16	23	30
Thursday	3	10	17	24	31
Friday	4	11	18	25	1
Saturday	5	12	19	26	2
Sunday	6	13	20	27	3
WEEK	9	10	11	12	13

Monday Montag Lundi Lunes Lunedì Segunda-feira Maandag 月

28

Tuesday Dienstag Mardi Martes Martedì Terça-feira Dinsdag 火

(ROK) Independence Movement Day

1

Wednesday Mittwoch Mercredi Miércoles Mercoledì Quarta-feira Woensdag 水

2

Thursday Donnerstag Jeudi Jueves Giovedì Quinta-feira Donderdag 木

◗

3

Friday Freitag Vendredi Viernes Venerdì Sexta-feira Vrijdag 金

4

Saturday Samstag Samedi Sábado Sabato Sábado Zaterdag 土

5

Sunday Sonntag Dimanche Domingo Domenica Domingo Zondag 日

6

10. WEEK

03.2005

Monday	7	14	21	28	4
Tuesday	8	15	22	29	5
Wednesday	9	16	23	30	6
Thursday	10	17	24	31	7
Friday	11	18	25	1	8
Saturday	12	19	26	2	9
Sunday	13	20	27	3	10
WEEK	**10**	**11**	**12**	**13**	**14**

Monday Montag Lundi Lunes Lunedì Segunda-feira Maandag 月

7

Tuesday Dienstag Mardi Martes Martedì Terça-feira Dinsdag 火

8

Wednesday Mittwoch Mercredi Miércoles Mercoledì Quarta-feira Woensdag 水

9

Thursday Donnerstag Jeudi Jueves Giovedì Quinta-feira Donderdag 木

●

10

Friday Freitag Vendredi Viernes Venerdì Sexta-feira Vrijdag 金

11

Saturday Samstag Samedi Sábado Sabato Sábado Zaterdag 土

12

Sunday Sonntag Dimanche Domingo Domenica Domingo Zondag 日

13

11. WEEK

03.2005

Monday Montag Lundi Lunes Lunedì Segunda-feira Maandag 月

14

Tuesday Dienstag Mardi Martes Martedì Terça-feira Dinsdag 火

15

Wednesday Mittwoch Mercredi Miércoles Mercoledì Quarta-feira Woensdag 水

16

Thursday Donnerstag Jeudi Jueves Giovedì Quinta-feira Donderdag 木

◗
(UK) Saint Patrick's Day
(Northern Ireland only)
(IRL) Saint Patrick's Day

17

Friday Freitag Vendredi Viernes Venerdì Sexta-feira Vrijdag 金

18

Saturday Samstag Samedi Sábado Sabato Sábado Zaterdag 土

19

Sunday Sonntag Dimanche Domingo Domenica Domingo Zondag 日

(J) Vernal Equinox Day

20

12. WEEK

03.2005

Monday	21	28	4	11	18
Tuesday	22	29	5	12	19
Wednesday	23	30	6	13	20
Thursday	24	31	7	14	21
Friday	25	1	8	15	22
Saturday	26	2	9	16	23
Sunday	27	3	10	17	24
WEEK	12	13	14	15	16

Monday Montag Lundi Lunes Lunedì Segunda-feira Maandag 月

(J) Public Holiday

21

Tuesday Dienstag Mardi Martes Martedì Terça-feira Dinsdag 火

22

Wednesday Mittwoch Mercredi Miércoles Mercoledì Quarta-feira Woensdag 水

23

Thursday Donnerstag Jeudi Jueves Giovedì Quinta-feira Donderdag 木

24

Friday Freitag Vendredi Viernes Venerdì Sexta-feira Vrijdag 金

○

25

(UK) (CDN) (D) (CH) (E) (P)
Good Friday | Vendredi Saint |
Karfreitag | Venerdì Santo |
Viernes Santo | Sexta-feira Santa
(IL) Purim

Saturday Samstag Samedi Sábado Sabato Sábado Zaterdag 土

26

Sunday Sonntag Dimanche Domingo Domenica Domingo Zondag 日

Easter Sunday | Pâques | Ostersonntag |
Pasqua | 1° Paasdag | Pascua |
Domingo de Páscoa

27

13. WEEK

03|04.2005

Monday	28	4	11	18	25
Tuesday	29	5	12	19	26
Wednesday	30	6	13	20	27
Thursday	31	7	14	21	28
Friday	1	8	15	22	29
Saturday	2	9	16	23	30
Sunday	3	10	17	24	1
WEEK	**13**	**14**	**15**	**16**	**17**

Monday Montag Lundi Lunes Lunedì Segunda-feira Maandag 月

28

(UK) Easter Monday (except Scotland)

(IRL) (CDN) (F) (D) (A) (CH) (NL) (I)

Easter Monday | Lundi de Pâques |
Ostermontag | Lunedì di Pasqua |
2e Paasdag | Lunedì dell'Angelo

Tuesday Dienstag Mardi Martes Martedì Terça-feira Dinsdag 火

29

Wednesday Mittwoch Mercredi Miércoles Mercoledì Quarta-feira Woensdag 水

30

Thursday Donnerstag Jeudi Jueves Giovedì Quinta-feira Donderdag 木

31

Friday Freitag Vendredi Viernes Venerdì Sexta-feira Vrijdag 金

1

Saturday Samstag Samedi Sábado Sabato Sábado Zaterdag 土

◗

2

Sunday Sonntag Dimanche Domingo Domenica Domingo Zondag 日

3

14. WEEK

04.2005

Monday	4	11	18	25	2
Tuesday	5	12	19	26	3
Wednesday	6	13	20	27	4
Thursday	7	14	21	28	5
Friday	8	15	22	29	6
Saturday	9	16	23	30	7
Sunday	10	17	24	1	8
WEEK	**14**	**15**	**16**	**17**	**18**

Monday Montag Lundi Lunes Lunedì Segunda-feira Maandag 月

4

Tuesday Dienstag Mardi Martes Martedì Terça-feira Dinsdag 火

(ROK) Arbor Day

5

Wednesday Mittwoch Mercredi Miércoles Mercoledì Quarta-feira Woensdag 水

6

Thursday Donnerstag Jeudi Jueves Giovedì Quinta-feira Donderdag 木

7

Friday Freitag Vendredi Viernes Venerdì Sexta-feira Vrijdag 金

●

8

Saturday Samstag Samedi Sábado Sabato Sábado Zaterdag 土

9

Sunday Sonntag Dimanche Domingo Domenica Domingo Zondag 日

10

15. WEEK

04.2005

Monday	11	18	25	2	9
Tuesday	12	19	26	3	10
Wednesday	13	20	27	4	11
Thursday	14	21	28	5	12
Friday	15	22	29	6	13
Saturday	16	23	30	7	14
Sunday	17	24	1	8	15
WEEK	**15**	**16**	**17**	**18**	**19**

Monday Montag Lundi Lunes Lunedì Segunda-feira Maandag 月

11

Tuesday Dienstag Mardi Martes Martedì Terça-feira Dinsdag 火

12

Wednesday Mittwoch Mercredi Miércoles Mercoledì Quarta-feira Woensdag 水

13

Thursday Donnerstag Jeudi Jueves Giovedì Quinta-feira Donderdag 木

14

Friday Freitag Vendredi Viernes Venerdì Sexta-feira Vrijdag 金

15

Saturday Samstag Samedi Sábado Sabato Sábado Zaterdag 土

16

Sunday Sonntag Dimanche Domingo Domenica Domingo Zondag 日

17

16. WEEK

04.2005

Monday	18	25	2	9	16
Tuesday	19	26	3	10	17
Wednesday	20	27	4	11	18
Thursday	21	28	5	12	19
Friday	22	29	6	13	20
Saturday	23	30	7	14	21
Sunday	24	1	8	15	22
WEEK	**16**	**17**	**18**	**19**	**20**

Monday Montag Lundi Lunes Lunedì Segunda-feira Maandag 月

18

Tuesday Dienstag Mardi Martes Martedì Terça-feira Dinsdag 火

19

Wednesday Mittwoch Mercredi Miércoles Mercoledì Quarta-feira Woensdag 水

20

Thursday Donnerstag Jeudi Jueves Giovedì Quinta-feira Donderdag 木

21

Friday Freitag Vendredi Viernes Venerdì Sexta-feira Vrijdag 金

22

Saturday Samstag Samedi Sábado Sabato Sábado Zaterdag 土

23

Sunday Sonntag Dimanche Domingo Domenica Domingo Zondag 日

○   (IL) Passover

24

17. WEEK

04|05.2005

Monday Montag Lundi Lunes Lunedì Segunda-feira Maandag 月

Ⓘ Liberazione
Ⓟ Dia da Liberdade

25

Tuesday Dienstag Mardi Martes Martedì Terça-feira Dinsdag 火

26

Wednesday Mittwoch Mercredi Miércoles Mercoledì Quarta-feira Woensdag 水

27

Thursday Donnerstag Jeudi Jueves Giovedì Quinta-feira Donderdag 木

28

Friday Freitag Vendredi Viernes Venerdì Sexta-feira Vrijdag 金

Ⓙ Greenery Day

29

Saturday Samstag Samedi Sábado Sabato Sábado Zaterdag 土

Ⓝⓛ Koninginnedag

30

Sunday Sonntag Dimanche Domingo Domenica Domingo Zondag 日

◑

Ⓕ Ⓓ Ⓐ Ⓘ Ⓟ
Fête du Travail | Maifeiertag |
Festa del Lavoro | Dia do Trabalhador
Ⓘⓛ Passover

1

18. ■ WEEK

05.2005

Monday	2	9	16	23	30
Tuesday	3	10	17	24	31
Wednesday	4	11	18	25	1
Thursday	5	12	19	26	2
Friday	6	13	20	27	3
Saturday	7	14	21	28	4
Sunday	8	15	22	29	5
WEEK	**18**	**19**	**20**	**21**	**22**

Monday Montag Lundi Lunes Lunedì Segunda-feira Maandag 月

(UK) (IRL)
Early May Bank Holiday
(E) Fiesta del Trabajo

2

Tuesday Dienstag Mardi Martes Martedì Terça-feira Dinsdag 火

(J) Constitution Day

3

Wednesday Mittwoch Mercredi Miércoles Mercoledì Quarta-feira Woensdag 水

(J) Public Holiday

4

Thursday Donnerstag Jeudi Jueves Giovedì Quinta-feira Donderdag 木

(F) (D) (A) (CH) (NL)
Ascension | Christi Himmelfahrt |
Auffahrt | Ascensione | Hemelvaartsdag
(J) (ROK) Children's Day
(IL) Yom Hashoah

5

Friday Freitag Vendredi Viernes Venerdì Sexta-feira Vrijdag 金

6

Saturday Samstag Samedi Sábado Sabato Sábado Zaterdag 土

7

Sunday Sonntag Dimanche Domingo Domenica Domingo Zondag 日

●

(F) Fête de la Libération

8

---

19. ■ WEEK

05.2005

Monday	9	16	23	30	6
Tuesday	10	17	24	31	7
Wednesday	11	18	25	1	8
Thursday	12	19	26	2	9
Friday	13	20	27	3	10
Saturday	14	21	28	4	11
Sunday	15	22	29	5	12
WEEK	**19**	**20**	**21**	**22**	**23**

Monday Montag Lundi Lunes Lunedì Segunda-feira Maandag 月

9

Tuesday Dienstag Mardi Martes Martedì Terça-feira Dinsdag 火

10

Wednesday Mittwoch Mercredi Miércoles Mercoledì Quarta-feira Woensdag 水

11

Thursday Donnerstag Jeudi Jueves Giovedì Quinta-feira Donderdag 木

(IL) Yom Haazmaut

12

Friday Freitag Vendredi Viernes Venerdì Sexta-feira Vrijdag 金

13

Saturday Samstag Samedi Sábado Sabato Sábado Zaterdag 土

14

Sunday Sonntag Dimanche Domingo Domenica Domingo Zondag 日

(F) (D) (A) (CH) (NL)
Pentecôte | Pfingstsonntag |
Pentecoste | 1º Pinksterdag
(ROK) Buddha's Birthday

15

20. WEEK

05.2005

Monday Montag Lundi Lunes Lunedì Segunda-feira Maandag 月

(D) (A) (CH) (NL)
Pfingstmontag | Lundi de Pentecôte |
Lunedì di Pentecoste | 2e Pinksterdag

16

Tuesday Dienstag Mardi Martes Martedì Terça-feira Dinsdag 火

17

Wednesday Mittwoch Mercredi Miércoles Mercoledì Quarta-feira Woensdag 水

18

Thursday Donnerstag Jeudi Jueves Giovedì Quinta-feira Donderdag 木

19

Friday Freitag Vendredi Viernes Venerdì Sexta-feira Vrijdag 金

20

Saturday Samstag Samedi Sábado Sabato Sábado Zaterdag 土

21

Sunday Sonntag Dimanche Domingo Domenica Domingo Zondag 日

22

21. WEEK

05.2005

Monday Montag Lundi Lunes Lunedì Segunda-feira Maandag 月

○   CDN Victoria Day | Fête de la Reine

23

Tuesday Dienstag Mardi Martes Martedì Terça-feira Dinsdag 火

24

Wednesday Mittwoch Mercredi Miércoles Mercoledì Quarta-feira Woensdag 水

25

Thursday Donnerstag Jeudi Jueves Giovedì Quinta-feira Donderdag 木

D Fronleichnam (teilweise)
A Fronleichnam
P Corpo de Deus

26

Friday Freitag Vendredi Viernes Venerdì Sexta-feira Vrijdag 金

27

Saturday Samstag Samedi Sábado Sabato Sábado Zaterdag 土

28

Sunday Sonntag Dimanche Domingo Domenica Domingo Zondag 日

29

22. WEEK

05|06.2005

Monday	30	6	13	20	27
Tuesday	31	7	14	21	28
Wednesday	1	8	15	22	29
Thursday	2	9	16	23	30
Friday	3	10	17	24	1
Saturday	4	11	18	25	2
Sunday	5	12	19	26	3
WEEK	**22**	**23**	**24**	**25**	**26**

Monday Montag Lundi Lunes Lunedì Segunda-feira Maandag 月

(USA) Memorial Day
(UK) Spring Bank Holiday

30

Tuesday Dienstag Mardi Martes Martedì Terça-feira Dinsdag 火

31

Wednesday Mittwoch Mercredi Miércoles Mercoledì Quarta-feira Woensdag 水

1

Thursday Donnerstag Jeudi Jueves Giovedì Quinta-feira Donderdag 木

(I) Festa della Repubblica

2

Friday Freitag Vendredi Viernes Venerdì Sexta-feira Vrijdag 金

3

Saturday Samstag Samedi Sábado Sabato Sábado Zaterdag 土

4

Sunday Sonntag Dimanche Domingo Domenica Domingo Zondag 日

5

23. WEEK

06.2005

Monday Montag Lundi Lunes Lunedì Segunda-feira Maandag 月

●

6

(IRL) First Monday in June
(ROK) Memorial Day

Tuesday Dienstag Mardi Martes Martedì Terça-feira Dinsdag 火

7

Wednesday Mittwoch Mercredi Miércoles Mercoledì Quarta-feira Woensdag 水

8

Thursday Donnerstag Jeudi Jueves Giovedì Quinta-feira Donderdag 木

9

Friday Freitag Vendredi Viernes Venerdì Sexta-feira Vrijdag 金

(P) Dia Nacional

10

Saturday Samstag Samedi Sábado Sabato Sábado Zaterdag 土

11

Sunday Sonntag Dimanche Domingo Domenica Domingo Zondag 日

12

24. WEEK

06.2005

Monday Montag Lundi Lunes Lunedì Segunda-feira Maandag 月

(IL) Shavuot

13

Tuesday Dienstag Mardi Martes Martedì Terça-feira Dinsdag 火

14

Wednesday Mittwoch Mercredi Miércoles Mercoledì Quarta-feira Woensdag 水

15

Thursday Donnerstag Jeudi Jueves Giovedì Quinta-feira Donderdag 木

16

Friday Freitag Vendredi Viernes Venerdì Sexta-feira Vrijdag 金

17

Saturday Samstag Samedi Sábado Sabato Sábado Zaterdag 土

18

Sunday Sonntag Dimanche Domingo Domenica Domingo Zondag 日

19

25. WEEK

06.2005

Monday Montag Lundi Lunes Lunedì Segunda-feira Maandag 月

20

Tuesday Dienstag Mardi Martes Martedì Terça-feira Dinsdag 火

21

Wednesday Mittwoch Mercredi Miércoles Mercoledì Quarta-feira Woensdag 水
○

22

Thursday Donnerstag Jeudi Jueves Giovedì Quinta-feira Donderdag 木

23

Friday Freitag Vendredi Viernes Venerdì Sexta-feira Vrijdag 金

24

Saturday Samstag Samedi Sábado Sabato Sábado Zaterdag 土

25

Sunday Sonntag Dimanche Domingo Domenica Domingo Zondag 日

26

26. ■ WEEK

06 | 07.2005

Monday	27	4	11	18	25
Tuesday	28	5	12	19	26
Wednesday	29	6	13	20	27
Thursday	30	7	14	21	28
Friday	1	8	15	22	29
Saturday	2	9	16	23	30
Sunday	3	10	17	24	31
WEEK	26	27	28	29	30

Monday Montag Lundi Lunes Lunedì Segunda-feira Maandag 月

27

Tuesday Dienstag Mardi Martes Martedì Terça-feira Dinsdag 火

◑

28

Wednesday Mittwoch Mercredi Miércoles Mercoledì Quarta-feira Woensdag 水

29

Thursday Donnerstag Jeudi Jueves Giovedì Quinta-feira Donderdag 木

30

Friday Freitag Vendredi Viernes Venerdì Sexta-feira Vrijdag 金

CDN Canada Day | Fête du Canada

1

Saturday Samstag Samedi Sábado Sabato Sábado Zaterdag 土

2

Sunday Sonntag Dimanche Domingo Domenica Domingo Zondag 日

3

27. ■ WEEK

07.2005

Monday	4	11	18	25	1
Tuesday	5	12	19	26	2
Wednesday	6	13	20	27	3
Thursday	7	14	21	28	4
Friday	8	15	22	29	5
Saturday	9	16	23	30	6
Sunday	10	17	24	31	7
WEEK	**27**	**28**	**29**	**30**	**31**

Monday Montag Lundi Lunes Lunedì Segunda-feira Maandag 月

(USA) Independence Day

4

Tuesday Dienstag Mardi Martes Martedì Terça-feira Dinsdag 火

5

Wednesday Mittwoch Mercredi Miércoles Mercoledì Quarta-feira Woensdag 水

6

Thursday Donnerstag Jeudi Jueves Giovedì Quinta-feira Donderdag 木

7

Friday Freitag Vendredi Viernes Venerdì Sexta-feira Vrijdag 金

8

Saturday Samstag Samedi Sábado Sabato Sábado Zaterdag 土

9

Sunday Sonntag Dimanche Domingo Domenica Domingo Zondag 日

10

28. WEEK

07.2005

Monday Montag Lundi Lunes Lunedì Segunda-feira Maandag 月

11

Tuesday Dienstag Mardi Martes Martedì Terça-feira Dinsdag 火

(UK) Battle of the Boyne Day
(Northern Ireland only)

12

Wednesday Mittwoch Mercredi Miércoles Mercoledì Quarta-feira Woensdag 水

13

Thursday Donnerstag Jeudi Jueves Giovedì Quinta-feira Donderdag 木

◗ (F) Fête Nationale

14

Friday Freitag Vendredi Viernes Venerdì Sexta-feira Vrijdag 金

15

Saturday Samstag Samedi Sábado Sabato Sábado Zaterdag 土

16

Sunday Sonntag Dimanche Domingo Domenica Domingo Zondag 日

(ROK) Constitution Day

17

29. ■ WEEK

07.2005

Monday Montag Lundi Lunes Lunedì Segunda-feira Maandag 月

Ⓙ Marine Day

18

Tuesday Dienstag Mardi Martes Martedì Terça-feira Dinsdag 火

19

Wednesday Mittwoch Mercredi Miércoles Mercoledì Quarta-feira Woensdag 水

20

Thursday Donnerstag Jeudi Jueves Giovedì Quinta-feira Donderdag 木
○

21

Friday Freitag Vendredi Viernes Venerdì Sexta-feira Vrijdag 金

22

Saturday Samstag Samedi Sábado Sabato Sábado Zaterdag 土

23

Sunday Sonntag Dimanche Domingo Domenica Domingo Zondag 日

24

30. WEEK

07.2005

Monday	25	1	8	15	22
Tuesday	26	2	9	16	23
Wednesday	27	3	10	17	24
Thursday	28	4	11	18	25
Friday	29	5	12	19	26
Saturday	30	6	13	20	27
Sunday	31	7	14	21	28
WEEK	**30**	**31**	**32**	**33**	**34**

Monday Montag Lundi Lunes Lunedì Segunda-feira Maandag 月

25

Tuesday Dienstag Mardi Martes Martedì Terça-feira Dinsdag 火

26

Wednesday Mittwoch Mercredi Miércoles Mercoledì Quarta-feira Woensdag 水

27

Thursday Donnerstag Jeudi Jueves Giovedì Quinta-feira Donderdag 木

◗

28

Friday Freitag Vendredi Viernes Venerdì Sexta-feira Vrijdag 金

29

Saturday Samstag Samedi Sábado Sabato Sábado Zaterdag 土

30

Sunday Sonntag Dimanche Domingo Domenica Domingo Zondag 日

31

31. ■ WEEK

08.2005

Monday	1	8	15	22	29
Tuesday	2	9	16	23	30
Wednesday	3	10	17	24	31
Thursday	4	11	18	25	1
Friday	5	12	19	26	2
Saturday	6	13	20	27	3
Sunday	7	14	21	28	4
WEEK	**31**	**32**	**33**	**34**	**35**

Monday Montag Lundi Lunes Lunedì Segunda-feira Maandag 月

1

(UK) Summer Bank Holiday
(Scotland only)
(IRL) First Monday in August
(CH) Bundesfeiertag | Fête nationale |
Festa nazionale

Tuesday Dienstag Mardi Martes Martedì Terça-feira Dinsdag 火

2

Wednesday Mittwoch Mercredi Miércoles Mercoledì Quarta-feira Woensdag 水

3

Thursday Donnerstag Jeudi Jueves Giovedì Quinta-feira Donderdag 木

4

Friday Freitag Vendredi Viernes Venerdì Sexta-feira Vrijdag 金

5

Saturday Samstag Samedi Sábado Sabato Sábado Zaterdag 土

6

Sunday Sonntag Dimanche Domingo Domenica Domingo Zondag 日

7

32. WEEK

08.2005

Monday Montag Lundi Lunes Lunedì Segunda-feira Maandag 月

8

Tuesday Dienstag Mardi Martes Martedì Terça-feira Dinsdag 火

9

Wednesday Mittwoch Mercredi Miércoles Mercoledì Quarta-feira Woensdag 水

10

Thursday Donnerstag Jeudi Jueves Giovedì Quinta-feira Donderdag 木

11

Friday Freitag Vendredi Viernes Venerdì Sexta-feira Vrijdag 金

12

Saturday Samstag Samedi Sábado Sabato Sábado Zaterdag 土

◑

13

Sunday Sonntag Dimanche Domingo Domenica Domingo Zondag 日

(IL) Tisha B'Av

14

33. WEEK

08.2005

Monday	15	22	29	5	12
Tuesday	16	23	30	6	13
Wednesday	17	24	31	7	14
Thursday	18	25	1	8	15
Friday	19	26	2	9	16
Saturday	20	27	3	10	17
Sunday	21	28	4	11	18
WEEK	33	34	35	36	37

Monday Montag Lundi Lunes Lunedì Segunda-feira Maandag 月

15

Ⓓ Mariä Himmelfahrt (teilweise)

Ⓕ Ⓐ Ⓔ Ⓘ Ⓟ
Assomption | Mariä Himmelfahrt |
Asunción de la Virgen | Assunzione |
Assunção de Nossa Senhora

ⓇⓄⓀ Independence Day

Tuesday Dienstag Mardi Martes Martedì Terça-feira Dinsdag 火

16

Wednesday Mittwoch Mercredi Miércoles Mercoledì Quarta-feira Woensdag 水

17

Thursday Donnerstag Jeudi Jueves Giovedì Quinta-feira Donderdag 木

18

Friday Freitag Vendredi Viernes Venerdì Sexta-feira Vrijdag 金

○

19

Saturday Samstag Samedi Sábado Sabato Sábado Zaterdag 土

20

Sunday Sonntag Dimanche Domingo Domenica Domingo Zondag 日

21

34. WEEK

08.2005

Monday	22	29	5	12	19
Tuesday	23	30	6	13	20
Wednesday	24	31	7	14	21
Thursday	25	1	8	15	22
Friday	26	2	9	16	23
Saturday	27	3	10	17	24
Sunday	28	4	11	18	25
WEEK	**34**	**35**	**36**	**37**	**38**

Monday Montag Lundi Lunes Lunedì Segunda-feira Maandag 月

22

Tuesday Dienstag Mardi Martes Martedì Terça-feira Dinsdag 火

23

Wednesday Mittwoch Mercredi Miércoles Mercoledì Quarta-feira Woensdag 水

24

Thursday Donnerstag Jeudi Jueves Giovedì Quinta-feira Donderdag 木

25

Friday Freitag Vendredi Viernes Venerdì Sexta-feira Vrijdag 金

26

Saturday Samstag Samedi Sábado Sabato Sábado Zaterdag 土

27

Sunday Sonntag Dimanche Domingo Domenica Domingo Zondag 日

28

35. ■ WEEK

08 | 09.2005

Monday	29	5	12	19	26
Tuesday	30	6	13	20	27
Wednesday	31	7	14	21	28
Thursday	1	8	15	22	29
Friday	2	9	16	23	30
Saturday	3	10	17	24	1
Sunday	4	11	18	25	2
WEEK	**35**	**36**	**37**	**38**	**39**

Monday Montag Lundi Lunes Lunedì Segunda-feira Maandag 月

(UK) Summer Bank Holiday
(except Scotland)

29

Tuesday Dienstag Mardi Martes Martedì Terça-feira Dinsdag 火

30

Wednesday Mittwoch Mercredi Miércoles Mercoledì Quarta-feira Woensdag 水

31

Thursday Donnerstag Jeudi Jueves Giovedì Quinta-feira Donderdag 木

1

Friday Freitag Vendredi Viernes Venerdì Sexta-feira Vrijdag 金

2

Saturday Samstag Samedi Sábado Sabato Sábado Zaterdag 土

●

3

Sunday Sonntag Dimanche Domingo Domenica Domingo Zondag 日

4

Dienes

36. WEEK

09.2005

Monday	5	12	19	26	3
Tuesday	6	13	20	27	4
Wednesday	7	14	21	28	5
Thursday	8	15	22	29	6
Friday	9	16	23	30	7
Saturday	10	17	24	1	8
Sunday	11	18	25	2	9
WEEK	**36**	**37**	**38**	**39**	**40**

Monday Montag Lundi Lunes Lunedì Segunda-feira Maandag 月

(USA) Labor Day
(CDN) Labour Day | Fête du Travail

5

Tuesday Dienstag Mardi Martes Martedì Terça-feira Dinsdag 火

6

Wednesday Mittwoch Mercredi Miércoles Mercoledì Quarta-feira Woensdag 水

7

Thursday Donnerstag Jeudi Jueves Giovedì Quinta-feira Donderdag 木

8

Friday Freitag Vendredi Viernes Venerdì Sexta-feira Vrijdag 金

9

Saturday Samstag Samedi Sábado Sabato Sábado Zaterdag 土

10

Sunday Sonntag Dimanche Domingo Domenica Domingo Zondag 日

◐

11

37. WEEK

09.2005

Monday	12	19	26	3	10
Tuesday	13	20	27	4	11
Wednesday	14	21	28	5	12
Thursday	15	22	29	6	13
Friday	16	23	30	7	14
Saturday	17	24	1	8	15
Sunday	18	25	2	9	16
WEEK	37	38	39	40	41

Monday Montag Lundi Lunes Lunedì Segunda-feira Maandag 月

12

Tuesday Dienstag Mardi Martes Martedì Terça-feira Dinsdag 火

13

Wednesday Mittwoch Mercredi Miércoles Mercoledì Quarta-feira Woensdag 水

14

Thursday Donnerstag Jeudi Jueves Giovedì Quinta-feira Donderdag 木

15

Friday Freitag Vendredi Viernes Venerdì Sexta-feira Vrijdag 金

16

Saturday Samstag Samedi Sábado Sabato Sábado Zaterdag 土

17

Sunday Sonntag Dimanche Domingo Domenica Domingo Zondag 日

○   (ROK) Chuseok

18

38. ■ WEEK

09.2005

Monday Montag Lundi Lunes Lunedì Segunda-feira Maandag 月

Ⓙ Respect-for-the-Aged Day

19

Tuesday Dienstag Mardi Martes Martedì Terça-feira Dinsdag 火

20

Wednesday Mittwoch Mercredi Miércoles Mercoledì Quarta-feira Woensdag 水

21

Thursday Donnerstag Jeudi Jueves Giovedì Quinta-feira Donderdag 木

22

Friday Freitag Vendredi Viernes Venerdì Sexta-feira Vrijdag 金

Ⓙ Autumn Equinox Day

23

Saturday Samstag Samedi Sábado Sabato Sábado Zaterdag 土

24

Sunday Sonntag Dimanche Domingo Domenica Domingo Zondag 日

◐

25

39. ■ WEEK

09|10.2005

	39	40	41	42	43
Monday	26	3	10	17	24
Tuesday	27	4	11	18	25
Wednesday	28	5	12	19	26
Thursday	29	6	13	20	27
Friday	30	7	14	21	28
Saturday	1	8	15	22	29
Sunday	2	9	16	23	30
WEEK	**39**	**40**	**41**	**42**	**43**

Monday Montag Lundi Lunes Lunedì Segunda-feira Maandag 月

26

Tuesday Dienstag Mardi Martes Martedì Terça-feira Dinsdag 火

27

Wednesday Mittwoch Mercredi Miércoles Mercoledì Quarta-feira Woensdag 水

28

Thursday Donnerstag Jeudi Jueves Giovedì Quinta-feira Donderdag 木

29

Friday Freitag Vendredi Viernes Venerdì Sexta-feira Vrijdag 金

30

Saturday Samstag Samedi Sábado Sabato Sábado Zaterdag 土

1

Sunday Sonntag Dimanche Domingo Domenica Domingo Zondag 日

2

40. WEEK

10.2005

Monday	3	10	17	24	31
Tuesday	4	11	18	25	1
Wednesday	5	12	19	26	2
Thursday	6	13	20	27	3
Friday	7	14	21	28	4
Saturday	8	15	22	29	5
Sunday	9	16	23	30	6
WEEK	**40**	**41**	**42**	**43**	**44**

Monday Montag Lundi Lunes Lunedì Segunda-feira Maandag 月

●

3

(D) Tag der Deutschen Einheit
(ROK) National Foundation Day

Tuesday Dienstag Mardi Martes Martedì Terça-feira Dinsdag 火

4

(IL) Rosh Hashanah

Wednesday Mittwoch Mercredi Miércoles Mercoledì Quarta-feira Woensdag 水

5

(P) Implantação da República
(IL) Rosh Hashanah

Thursday Donnerstag Jeudi Jueves Giovedì Quinta-feira Donderdag 木

6

Friday Freitag Vendredi Viernes Venerdì Sexta-feira Vrijdag 金

7

Saturday Samstag Samedi Sábado Sabato Sábado Zaterdag 土

8

Sunday Sonntag Dimanche Domingo Domenica Domingo Zondag 日

9

41. WEEK

10.2005

Monday	10	17	24	31	7
Tuesday	11	18	25	1	8
Wednesday	12	19	26	2	9
Thursday	13	20	27	3	10
Friday	14	21	28	4	11
Saturday	15	22	29	5	12
Sunday	16	23	30	6	13
WEEK	41	42	43	44	45

Monday Montag Lundi Lunes Lunedì Segunda-feira Maandag 月

◖

USA Columbus Day

CDN Thanksgiving Day | Action de Grâces

J Health-Sports Day

10

Tuesday Dienstag Mardi Martes Martedì Terça-feira Dinsdag 火

11

Wednesday Mittwoch Mercredi Miércoles Mercoledì Quarta-feira Woensdag 水

E Fiesta Nacional

12

Thursday Donnerstag Jeudi Jueves Giovedì Quinta-feira Donderdag 木

IL Yom Kippur

13

Friday Freitag Vendredi Viernes Venerdì Sexta-feira Vrijdag 金

14

Saturday Samstag Samedi Sábado Sabato Sábado Zaterdag 土

15

Sunday Sonntag Dimanche Domingo Domenica Domingo Zondag 日

16

42. WEEK

10.2005

Monday	17	24	31	7	14
Tuesday	18	25	1	8	15
Wednesday	19	26	2	9	16
Thursday	20	27	3	10	17
Friday	21	28	4	11	18
Saturday	22	29	5	12	19
Sunday	23	30	6	13	20
WEEK	**42**	**43**	**44**	**45**	**46**

Monday Montag Lundi Lunes Lunedì Segunda-feira Maandag 月

○

17

Tuesday Dienstag Mardi Martes Martedì Terça-feira Dinsdag 火

(IL) Succoth

18

Wednesday Mittwoch Mercredi Miércoles Mercoledì Quarta-feira Woensdag 水

19

Thursday Donnerstag Jeudi Jueves Giovedì Quinta-feira Donderdag 木

20

Friday Freitag Vendredi Viernes Venerdì Sexta-feira Vrijdag 金

21

Saturday Samstag Samedi Sábado Sabato Sábado Zaterdag 土

22

Sunday Sonntag Dimanche Domingo Domenica Domingo Zondag 日

23

43. WEEK

10.2005

Monday Montag Lundi Lunes Lunedì Segunda-feira Maandag 月

24

Tuesday Dienstag Mardi Martes Martedì Terça-feira Dinsdag 火

Ⓘ Sh'mini Atzereth

25

Wednesday Mittwoch Mercredi Miércoles Mercoledì Quarta-feira Woensdag 水

Ⓐ Nationalfeiertag
Ⓘ Simchat Torah

26

Thursday Donnerstag Jeudi Jueves Giovedì Quinta-feira Donderdag 木

27

Friday Freitag Vendredi Viernes Venerdì Sexta-feira Vrijdag 金

28

Saturday Samstag Samedi Sábado Sabato Sábado Zaterdag 土

29

Sunday Sonntag Dimanche Domingo Domenica Domingo Zondag 日

30

44. WEEK

10|11.2005

Monday	31	7	14	21	28
Tuesday	1	8	15	22	29
Wednesday	2	9	16	23	30
Thursday	3	10	17	24	1
Friday	4	11	18	25	2
Saturday	5	12	19	26	3
Sunday	6	13	20	27	4
WEEK	**44**	**45**	**46**	**47**	**48**

Monday Montag Lundi Lunes Lunedì Segunda-feira Maandag 月

(IRL) Last Monday in October
(D) Reformationstag (teilweise)

31

Tuesday Dienstag Mardi Martes Martedì Terça-feira Dinsdag 火

(D) Allerheiligen (teilweise)
(F) (A) (E) (I) (P)
Toussaint | Allerheiligen | Todos los
Santos | Ognissanti | Todos os Santos

1

Wednesday Mittwoch Mercredi Miércoles Mercoledì Quarta-feira Woensdag 水

●

2

Thursday Donnerstag Jeudi Jueves Giovedì Quinta-feira Donderdag 木

(J) Culture Day

3

Friday Freitag Vendredi Viernes Venerdì Sexta-feira Vrijdag 金

4

Saturday Samstag Samedi Sábado Sabato Sábado Zaterdag 土

5

Sunday Sonntag Dimanche Domingo Domenica Domingo Zondag 日

6

---

45. WEEK

11.2005

Monday	7	14	21	28	5
Tuesday	8	15	22	29	6
Wednesday	9	16	23	30	7
Thursday	10	17	24	1	8
Friday	11	18	25	2	9
Saturday	12	19	26	3	10
Sunday	13	20	27	4	11
WEEK	**45**	**46**	**47**	**48**	**49**

Monday Montag Lundi Lunes Lunedì Segunda-feira Maandag 月

7

Tuesday Dienstag Mardi Martes Martedì Terça-feira Dinsdag 火

8

Wednesday Mittwoch Mercredi Miércoles Mercoledì Quarta-feira Woensdag 水

9

Thursday Donnerstag Jeudi Jueves Giovedì Quinta-feira Donderdag 木

10

Friday Freitag Vendredi Viernes Venerdì Sexta-feira Vrijdag 金

11

(USA) Veterans' Day
(CDN) Remembrance Day | Jour du Souvenir
(F) Armistice 1918

Saturday Samstag Samedi Sábado Sabato Sábado Zaterdag 土

12

Sunday Sonntag Dimanche Domingo Domenica Domingo Zondag 日

13

46. WEEK

11.2005

Monday Montag Lundi Lunes Lunedì Segunda-feira Maandag 月

14

Tuesday Dienstag Mardi Martes Martedì Terça-feira Dinsdag 火

15

Wednesday Mittwoch Mercredi Miércoles Mercoledì Quarta-feira Woensdag 水

○   Ⓓ Buß- und Bettag (teilweise)

16

Thursday Donnerstag Jeudi Jueves Giovedì Quinta-feira Donderdag 木

17

Friday Freitag Vendredi Viernes Venerdì Sexta-feira Vrijdag 金

18

Saturday Samstag Samedi Sábado Sabato Sábado Zaterdag 土

19

Sunday Sonntag Dimanche Domingo Domenica Domingo Zondag 日

20

47. WEEK

11.2005

Monday	21	28	5	12	19
Tuesday	22	29	6	13	20
Wednesday	23	30	7	14	21
Thursday	24	1	8	15	22
Friday	25	2	9	16	23
Saturday	26	3	10	17	24
Sunday	27	4	11	18	25
WEEK	**47**	**48**	**49**	**50**	**51**

Monday Montag Lundi Lunes Lunedì Segunda-feira Maandag 月

21

Tuesday Dienstag Mardi Martes Martedì Terça-feira Dinsdag 火

22

Wednesday Mittwoch Mercredi Miércoles Mercoledì Quarta-feira Woensdag 水

◑   (J) Labor-Thanksgiving Day

23

Thursday Donnerstag Jeudi Jueves Giovedì Quinta-feira Donderdag 木

(USA) Thanksgiving Day

24

Friday Freitag Vendredi Viernes Venerdì Sexta-feira Vrijdag 金

25

Saturday Samstag Samedi Sábado Sabato Sábado Zaterdag 土

26

Sunday Sonntag Dimanche Domingo Domenica Domingo Zondag 日

27

48. WEEK

11|12.2005

Monday Montag Lundi Lunes Lunedì Segunda-feira Maandag 月

28

Tuesday Dienstag Mardi Martes Martedì Terça-feira Dinsdag 火

29

Wednesday Mittwoch Mercredi Miércoles Mercoledì Quarta-feira Woensdag 水

30

Thursday Donnerstag Jeudi Jueves Giovedì Quinta-feira Donderdag 木

●   Ⓟ Dia da Restauração

1

Friday Freitag Vendredi Viernes Venerdì Sexta-feira Vrijdag 金

2

Saturday Samstag Samedi Sábado Sabato Sábado Zaterdag 土

3

Sunday Sonntag Dimanche Domingo Domenica Domingo Zondag 日

4

49. ∎ WEEK

12.2005

Monday	5	12	19	26	2
Tuesday	6	13	20	27	3
Wednesday	7	14	21	28	4
Thursday	8	15	22	29	5
Friday	9	16	23	30	6
Saturday	10	17	24	31	7
Sunday	11	18	25	1	8
WEEK	**49**	**50**	**51**	**52**	**1**

Monday Montag Lundi Lunes Lunedì Segunda-feira Maandag 月

5

Tuesday Dienstag Mardi Martes Martedì Terça-feira Dinsdag 火

(E) Día de la Constitución

6

Wednesday Mittwoch Mercredi Miércoles Mercoledì Quarta-feira Woensdag 水

7

Thursday Donnerstag Jeudi Jueves Giovedì Quinta-feira Donderdag 木

(A) (E) (I) (P)
Mariä Empfängnis | Inmaculada
Concepción | Immacolata Concezione |
Imaculada Conceição

8

Friday Freitag Vendredi Viernes Venerdì Sexta-feira Vrijdag 金

9

Saturday Samstag Samedi Sábado Sabato Sábado Zaterdag 土

10

Sunday Sonntag Dimanche Domingo Domenica Domingo Zondag 日

11

50. WEEK

12.2005

Monday	12	19	26	2	9
Tuesday	13	20	27	3	10
Wednesday	14	21	28	4	11
Thursday	15	22	29	5	12
Friday	16	23	30	6	13
Saturday	17	24	31	7	14
Sunday	18	25	1	8	15
WEEK	**50**	**51**	**52**	**1**	**2**

Monday Montag Lundi Lunes Lunedì Segunda-feira Maandag 月

12

Tuesday Dienstag Mardi Martes Martedì Terça-feira Dinsdag 火

13

Wednesday Mittwoch Mercredi Miércoles Mercoledì Quarta-feira Woensdag 水

14

Thursday Donnerstag Jeudi Jueves Giovedì Quinta-feira Donderdag 木
○

15

Friday Freitag Vendredi Viernes Venerdì Sexta-feira Vrijdag 金

16

Saturday Samstag Samedi Sábado Sabato Sábado Zaterdag 土

17

Sunday Sonntag Dimanche Domingo Domenica Domingo Zondag 日

18

51. WEEK

12.2005

Monday	19	26	2	9	16
Tuesday	20	27	3	10	17
Wednesday	21	28	4	11	18
Thursday	22	29	5	12	19
Friday	23	30	6	13	20
Saturday	24	31	7	14	21
Sunday	25	1	8	15	22
WEEK	51	52	1	2	3

Monday Montag Lundi Lunes Lunedì Segunda-feira Maandag 月

19

Tuesday Dienstag Mardi Martes Martedì Terça-feira Dinsdag 火

20

Wednesday Mittwoch Mercredi Miércoles Mercoledì Quarta-feira Woensdag 水

21

Thursday Donnerstag Jeudi Jueves Giovedì Quinta-feira Donderdag 木

22

Friday Freitag Vendredi Viernes Venerdì Sexta-feira Vrijdag 金

◗   (J) Emperor's Birthday

23

Saturday Samstag Samedi Sábado Sabato Sábado Zaterdag 土

24

Sunday Sonntag Dimanche Domingo Domenica Domingo Zondag 日

(USA) (UK) (IRL) (ROK) (CDN) (F) (D) (A) (CH)
(NL) (E) (I) (P)
Christmas Day | Noël | 1. Weihnachtstag |
Weihnachten | 1e Kerstdag | Natividad
del Señor | Natale | Dia de Natal

25

52. WEEK   12.2005 | 01.2006

Monday	26	2	9	16	23
Tuesday	27	3	10	17	24
Wednesday	28	4	11	18	25
Thursday	29	5	12	19	26
Friday	30	6	13	20	27
Saturday	31	7	14	21	28
Sunday	1	8	15	22	29
WEEK	52	1	2	3	4

Monday Montag Lundi Lunes Lunedì Segunda-feira Maandag 月

26

(UK) (IRL) (CDN) (D) (A) (CH) (NL) (I)
Boxing Day | Saint Stephen's Day |
Lendemain de Noël | 2. Weihnachtstag |
Stefanstag | S. Etienne | 2ᵉ Kerstdag |
S. Stefano
(IL) Hanukkah

Tuesday Dienstag Mardi Martes Martedì Terça-feira Dinsdag 火

27

(UK) Public Holiday

Wednesday Mittwoch Mercredi Miércoles Mercoledì Quarta-feira Woensdag 水

28

Thursday Donnerstag Jeudi Jueves Giovedì Quinta-feira Donderdag 木

29

Friday Freitag Vendredi Viernes Venerdì Sexta-feira Vrijdag 金

30

Saturday Samstag Samedi Sábado Sabato Sábado Zaterdag 土
●

31

Sunday Sonntag Dimanche Domingo Domenica Domingo Zondag 日

New Year's Day | Jour de l'An | Neujahr |
Nieuwjaarsdag | Nieuwjaar | Nouvel An |
Capodanno

1

PUBLIC HOLIDAYS 2005

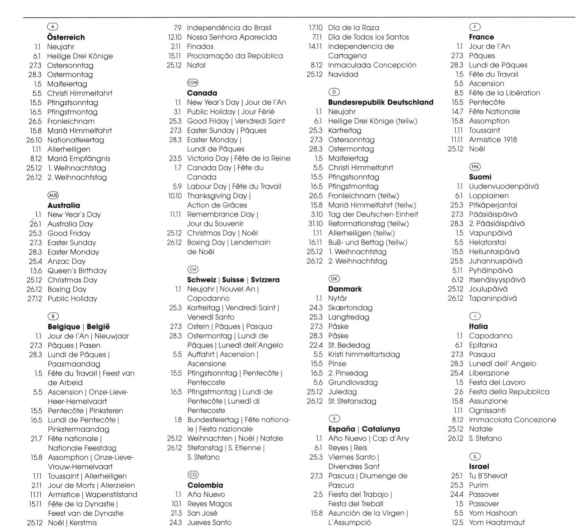

(A) Österreich
- 1.1 Neujahr
- 6.1 Heilige Drei Könige
- 27.3 Ostersonntag
- 28.3 Ostermontag
- 1.5 Maifeiertag
- 5.5 Christi Himmelfahrt
- 15.5 Pfingstsonntag
- 16.5 Pfingstmontag
- 26.5 Fronleichnam
- 15.8 Mariä Himmelfahrt
- 26.10 Nationalfeiertag
- 1.11 Allerheiligen
- 8.12 Mariä Empfängnis
- 25.12 1. Weihnachtstag
- 26.12 2. Weihnachtstag

(AUS) Australia
- 1.1 New Year's Day
- 26.1 Australia Day
- 25.3 Good Friday
- 27.3 Easter Sunday
- 28.3 Easter Monday
- 25.4 Anzac Day
- 13.6 Queen's Birthday
- 25.12 Christmas Day
- 26.12 Boxing Day
- 27.12 Public Holiday

(B) Belgique | België
- 1.1 Jour de l'An | Nieuwjaar
- 27.3 Pâques | Pasen
- 28.3 Lundi de Pâques | Paasmaandag
- 1.5 Fête du Travail | Feest van de Arbeid
- 5.5 Ascension | Onze-Lieve-Heer-Hemelvaart
- 15.5 Pentecôte | Pinksteren
- 16.5 Lundi de Pentecôte | Pinkstermaandag
- 21.7 Fête nationale | Nationale Feestdag
- 15.8 Assomption | Onze-Lieve-Vrouw-Hemelvaart
- 1.11 Toussaint | Allerheiligen
- 2.11 Jour de Morts | Allerzielen
- 11.11 Armistice | Wapenstilstand
- 15.11 Fête de la Dynastie | Feest van de Dynastie
- 25.12 Noël | Kerstmis

(BR) Brasil
- 1.1 Ano Novo
- 8.2 Carnaval
- 25.3 Sexta-feira da Paixão
- 27.3 Páscoa
- 21.4 Tiradentes
- 1.5 Dia do Trabalho
- 26.5 Corpus Christi
- 7.9 Independência do Brasil
- 12.10 Nossa Senhora Aparecida
- 2.11 Finados
- 15.11 Proclamação da República
- 25.12 Natal

(CDN) Canada
- 1.1 New Year's Day | Jour de l'An
- 3.1 Public Holiday | Jour Férié
- 25.3 Good Friday | Vendredi Saint
- 27.3 Easter Sunday | Pâques
- 28.3 Easter Monday | Lundi de Pâques
- 23.5 Victoria Day | Fête de la Reine
- 1.7 Canada Day | Fête du Canada
- 5.9 Labour Day | Fête du Travail
- 10.10 Thanksgiving Day | Action de Grâces
- 11.11 Remembrance Day | Jour du Souvenir
- 25.12 Christmas Day | Noël
- 26.12 Boxing Day | Lendemain de Noël

(CH) Schweiz | Suisse | Svizzera
- 1.1 Neujahr | Nouvel An | Capodanno
- 25.3 Karfreitag | Vendredi Saint | Venerdì Santo
- 27.3 Ostern | Pâques | Pasqua
- 28.3 Ostermontag | Lundi de Pâques | Lunedì dell'Angelo
- 5.5 Auffahrt | Ascension | Ascensione
- 15.5 Pfingstsonntag | Pentecôte | Pentecoste
- 16.5 Pfingstmontag | Lundi de Pentecôte | Lunedì di Pentecoste
- 1.8 Bundesfeiertag | Fête nationale | Festa nazionale
- 25.12 Weihnachten | Noël | Natale
- 26.12 Stefanstag | S. Etienne | S. Stefano

(CO) Colombia
- 1.1 Año Nuevo
- 10.1 Reyes Magos
- 21.3 San José
- 24.3 Jueves Santo
- 25.3 Viernes Santo
- 27.3 Pascua
- 1.5 Día del Trabajo
- 9.5 Ascención del Señor
- 30.5 Corpus Christi
- 6.6 Sagrado Corazón
- 4.7 San Pedro y San Pablo
- 20.7 Independencia Nacional
- 7.8 Batalla de Boyacá
- 15.8 Asunción de la Virgen
- 17.10 Día de la Raza
- 7.11 Día de Todos los Santos
- 14.11 Independencia de Cartagena
- 8.12 Inmaculada Concepción
- 25.12 Navidad

(D) Bundesrepublik Deutschland
- 1.1 Neujahr
- 6.1 Heilige Drei Könige (teilw.)
- 25.3 Karfreitag
- 27.3 Ostersonntag
- 28.3 Ostermontag
- 1.5 Maifeiertag
- 5.5 Christi Himmelfahrt
- 15.5 Pfingstsonntag
- 16.5 Pfingstmontag
- 26.5 Fronleichnam (teilw.)
- 15.8 Mariä Himmelfahrt (teilw.)
- 3.10 Tag der Deutschen Einheit
- 31.10 Reformationstag (teilw.)
- 1.11 Allerheiligen (teilw.)
- 16.11 Buß- und Bettag (teilw.)
- 25.12 1. Weihnachtstag
- 26.12 2. Weihnachtstag

(DK) Danmark
- 1.1 Nytår
- 24.3 Skærtorsdag
- 25.3 Langfredag
- 27.3 Påske
- 28.3 Påske
- 22.4 St. Bededag
- 5.5 Kristi himmelfartsdag
- 15.5 Pinse
- 16.5 2. Pinsedag
- 5.6 Grundlovsdag
- 25.12 Juledag
- 26.12 St. Stefansdag

(E) España | Catalunya
- 1.1 Año Nuevo | Cap d'Any
- 6.1 Reyes | Reis
- 25.3 Viernes Santo | Divendres Sant
- 27.3 Pascua | Diumenge de Pascua
- 2.5 Fiesta del Trabajo | Festa del Treball
- 15.8 Asunción de la Virgen | L'Assumpció
- 12.10 Fiesta Nacional | Festa Nacional d'Espanya
- 1.11 Todos los Santos | Tots Sants
- 6.12 Día de la Constitución | Dia de la Constitució
- 8.12 Inmaculada Concepción | La Immaculada
- 25.12 Natividad del Señor | Nadal

(F) France
- 1.1 Jour de l'An
- 27.3 Pâques
- 28.3 Lundi de Pâques
- 1.5 Fête du Travail
- 5.5 Ascension
- 8.5 Fête de la Libération
- 15.5 Pentecôte
- 14.7 Fête Nationale
- 15.8 Assomption
- 1.11 Toussaint
- 11.11 Armistice 1918
- 25.12 Noël

(FIN) Suomi
- 1.1 Uudenvuodenpäivä
- 6.1 Loppiainen
- 25.3 Pitkäperjantai
- 27.3 Pääsiäispäivä
- 28.3 2. Pääsiäispäivä
- 1.5 Vapunpäivä
- 5.5 Helatorstai
- 15.5 Helluntaipäivä
- 25.5 Juhannuspäivä
- 5.11 Pyhäinpäivä
- 6.12 Itsenäisyyspäivä
- 25.12 Joulupäivä
- 26.12 Tapaninpäivä

(I) Italia
- 1.1 Capodanno
- 6.1 Epifania
- 27.3 Pasqua
- 28.3 Lunedì dell' Angelo
- 25.4 Liberazione
- 1.5 Festa del Lavoro
- 2.6 Festa della Repubblica
- 15.8 Assunzione
- 1.11 Ognissanti
- 8.12 Immacolata Concezione
- 25.12 Natale
- 26.12 S. Stefano

(IL) Israel
- 25.1 Tu B'Shevat
- 25.3 Purim
- 24.4 Passover
- 1.5 Passover
- 5.5 Yom Hashoah
- 12.5 Yom Haatzmaut
- 13.6 Shavuot
- 14.8 Tisha B'Av
- 4.10 Rosh Hashanah
- 5.10 Rosh Hashanah
- 13.10 Yom Kippur
- 18.10 Succoth
- 25.10 Sh'mini Atzereth
- 26.10 Simchat Torah
- 26.12 Hanukkah

PUBLIC HOLIDAYS 2005

(IRL) Ireland
1.1	New Year's Day
17.3	Saint Patrick's Day
27.3	Easter Sunday
28.3	Easter Monday
2.5	First Monday in May
6.6	First Monday in June
1.8	First Monday in August
31.10	Last Monday in October
25.12	Christmas Day
26.12	Saint Stephen's Day

(J) Japan
1.1	New Year's Day
10.1	Coming-of-Age Day
11.2	Commemoration of the Founding of the Nation
20.3	Vernal Equinox Day
21.3	Public Holiday
29.4	Greenery Day
3.5	Constitution Day
4.5	Public Holiday
5.5	Children's Day
18.7	Marine Day
19.9	Respect-for-the-Aged Day
23.9	Autumn Equinox Day
10.10	Health-Sports Day
3.11	Culture Day
23.11	Labor-Thanksgiving Day
23.12	Emperor's Birthday

(L) Luxembourg
1.1	Jour de l'An
27.3	Pâques
28.3	Lundi de Pâques
1.5	Fête du Travail
5.5	Ascension
15.5	Pentecôte
16.5	Lundi de Pentecôte
23.6	Fête Nationale
15.8	Assomption
1.11	Toussaint
25.12	Noël
26.12	Lendemain de Noël

(MEX) México
1.1	Año Nuevo
5.2	Aniversario de la Constitución
21.3	Natalicio de Benito Juárez
24.3	Jueves Santo
25.3	Viernes Santo
27.3	Pascua
1.5	Día del Trabajo
1.9	Informe presidencial
16.9	Día de la Independencia
20.11	Aniversario de la Revolución Mexicana
25.12	Navidad

(N) Norge
1.1	Nyttårsdag
20.3	Palmesøndag
24.3	Skjærtorsdag
25.3	Langfredag
27.3	1. påskedag
28.3	2. påskedag
1.5	Offentlig høytidsdag
17.5	Grunnlovsdag
5.5	Kristi himmelfartsdag
15.5	1. pinsedag
16.5	2. pinsedag
25.12	1. juledag
26.12	2. juledag

(NL) Nederland
1.1	Nieuwjaarsdag
27.3	1e Paasdag
28.3	2e Paasdag
30.4	Koninginnedag
5.5	Hemelvaartsdag
15.5	1e Pinksterdag
16.5	2e Pinksterdag
25.12	1e Kerstdag
26.12	2e Kerstdag

(NZ) New Zealand
1.1	New Year's Day
2.1	Day after New Year's Day
6.2	Waitangi Day
25.3	Good Friday
27.3	Easter Sunday
28.3	Easter Monday
25.4	Anzac Day
6.6	Queen's Birthday
24.10	Labour Day
25.12	Christmas Day
26.12	Boxing Day
27.12	Public Holiday

(P) Portugal
1.1	Ano Novo
25.3	Sexta-feira Santa
27.3	Domingo de Páscoa
25.4	Dia da Liberdade
1.5	Dia do Trabalhador
26.5	Corpo de Deus
10.6	Dia Nacional
15.8	Assunção de Nossa Senhora
5.10	Implantação da República
1.11	Todos os Santos
1.12	Dia da Restauração
8.12	Imaculada Conceição
25.12	Dia de Natal

(RA) Argentina
1.1	Año Nuevo
24.3	Jueves Santo
25.3	Viernes Santo
27.3	Pascua
4.4	Recuperación de las Islas Malvinas
1.5	Día del Trabajador
25.5	Fundación del Primer Gobierno Nacional
20.6	Día de la Bandera
9.7	Día de la Independencia
17.8	Muerte del General San Martín
12.10	Descubrimiento de América
8.12	Inmaculada Concepción de la Virgen María
25.12	Navidad

(RCH) Chile
1.1	Año Nuevo
25.3	Viernes Santo
27.3	Pascua
1.5	Día del Trabajo
21.5	Combate Naval de Iquique
23.5	Corpus Christi
15.8	Asunción de la Virgen
18.9	Fiestas Patrias
19.9	Día del Ejército
12.10	Día de la Hispanidad
1.11	Todos los Santos
8.12	Inmaculada Concepción
25.12	Navidad

(ROK) Korea
1.1	New Year's Day
1.3	Independence Movement Day
5.4	Arbor Day
5.5	Children's Day
15.5	Buddha's Birthday
6.6	Memorial Day
17.7	Constitution Day
15.8	Independence Day
18.9	Chuseok
3.10	National Foundation Day
25.12	Christmas Day

(S) Sverige
1.1	Nyårsdagen
6.1	Trettondedag jul
25.3	Långfredagen
27.3	Påskdagen
28.3	Annandag påsk
1.5	Första maj
5.5	Kristi himmelsfärds dag
15.5	Pingstdagen
16.5	Annandag pingst
25.6	Midsommardagen
5.11	Alla helgons dag
25.12	Juldagen
26.12	Annandag jul

(UK) United Kingdom
1.1	New Year's Day
3.1	Public Holiday
4.1	Public Holiday (Scotland only)
17.3	Saint Patrick's Day (Northern Ireland only)
25.3	Good Friday
27.3	Easter Sunday
28.3	Easter Monday (except Scotland)
2.5	May Bank Holiday
30.5	Spring Bank Holiday
12.7	Battle of the Boyne Day (Northern Ireland only)
1.8	Summer Bank Holiday (Scotland only)
29.8	Summer Bank Holiday (except Scotland)
25.12	Christmas Day
26.12	Boxing Day
27.12	Public Holiday

(USA) United States
1.1	New Year's Day
17.1	Martin Luther King Day
21.2	President's Day
27.3	Easter Sunday
30.5	Memorial Day
4.7	Independence Day
5.9	Labor Day
10.10	Columbus Day
11.11	Veterans' Day
24.11	Thanksgiving Day
25.12	Christmas Day

(ZA) South Africa
1.1	New Year's Day
21.3	Human Rights Day
25.3	Good Friday
27.3	Easter Sunday
28.3	Family Day
27.4	Freedom Day
1.5	Workers' Day
2.5	Public Holiday
16.6	Youth Day
9.8	National Women's Day
24.9	Heritage Day
16.12	Day of Reconciliation
25.12	Christmas Day
26.12	Day of Goodwill

Some international holidays may be subject to change.

01–04.2006

YEAR PLANNER

JANUARY	FEBRUARY	MARCH	APRIL
1 Su	1 We	1 We	1 Sa
WEEK 1	2 Th	2 Th	2 Su
2 Mo	3 Fr	3 Fr	**WEEK 14**
3 Tu	4 Sa	4 Sa	3 Mo
4 We	5 Su ◑	5 Su	4 Tu
5 Th	**WEEK 6**	**WEEK 10**	5 We ◐
6 Fr ◐	6 Mo	6 Mo ◐	6 Th
7 Sa	7 Tu	7 Tu	7 Fr
8 Su	8 We	8 We	8 Sa
WEEK 2	9 Th	9 Th	9 Su
9 Mo	10 Fr	10 Fr	**WEEK 15**
10 Tu	11 Sa	11 Sa	10 Mo
11 We	12 Su	12 Su	11 Tu
12 Th	**WEEK 7**	**WEEK 11**	12 We
13 Fr	13 Mo ○	13 Mo	13 Th ○
14 Sa ○	14 Tu	14 Tu ○	14 Fr
15 Su	15 We	15 We	15 Sa
WEEK 3	16 Th	16 Th	16 Su
16 Mo	17 Fr	17 Fr	**WEEK 16**
17 Tu	18 Sa	18 Sa	17 Mo
18 We	19 Su	19 Su	18 Tu
19 Th	**WEEK 8**	**WEEK 12**	19 We
20 Fr	20 Mo	20 Mo	20 Th
21 Sa	21 Tu ◑	21 Tu	21 Fr ◑
22 Su ◑	22 We	22 We ◑	22 Sa
WEEK 4	23 Th ○	23 Th	23 Su
23 Mo	24 Fr	24 Fr	**WEEK 17**
24 Tu	25 Sa	25 Sa	24 Mo
25 We	26 Su	26 Su	25 Tu
26 Th	**WEEK 9**	**WEEK 13**	26 We
27 Fr	27 Mo	27 Mo	27 Th ●
28 Sa	28 Tu ●	28 Tu	28 Fr
29 Su ●		29 We ●	29 Sa
WEEK 5		30 Th	30 Su
30 Mo		31 Fr	
31 Tu			

05–08.2006

MAY

WEEK 18

1 Mo
2 Tu
3 We
4 Th
5 Fr ☾
6 Sa
7 Su

WEEK 19

8 Mo
9 Tu
10 We
11 Th
12 Fr
13 Sa ○
14 Su

WEEK 20

15 Mo
16 Tu
17 We
18 Th
19 Fr
20 Sa ☽
21 Su

WEEK 21

22 Mo
23 Tu
24 We
25 Th
26 Fr
27 Sa ●
28 Su

WEEK 22

29 Mo
30 Tu
31 We

JUNE

1 Th
2 Fr
3 Sa ☾
4 Su

WEEK 23

5 Mo
6 Tu
7 We
8 Th
9 Fr
10 Sa
11 Su ○

WEEK 24

12 Mo
13 Tu
14 We
15 Th
16 Fr
17 Sa
18 Su ☽

WEEK 25

19 Mo
20 Tu
21 We
22 Th
23 Fr
24 Sa
25 Su ●

WEEK 26

26 Mo
27 Tu
28 We
29 Th
30 Fr

JULY

1 Sa
2 Su

WEEK 27

3 Mo ☾
4 Tu
5 We
6 Th
7 Fr
8 Sa
9 Su

WEEK 28

10 Mo
11 Tu ○
12 We
13 Th
14 Fr
15 Sa
16 Su

WEEK 29

17 Mo ☽
18 Tu
19 We
20 Th
21 Fr
22 Sa
23 Su

WEEK 30

24 Mo
25 Tu ●
26 We
27 Th
28 Fr
29 Sa
30 Su

WEEK 31

31 Mo

AUGUST

1 Tu
2 We ☾
3 Th
4 Fr
5 Sa
6 Su

WEEK 32

7 Mo
8 Tu
9 We ○
10 Th
11 Fr
12 Sa
13 Su

WEEK 33

14 Mo
15 Tu
16 We ☽
17 Th
18 Fr
19 Sa
20 Su

WEEK 34

21 Mo
22 Tu
23 We ●
24 Th
25 Fr
26 Sa
27 Su

WEEK 35

28 Mo
29 Tu
30 We
31 Th ☾

09–12.2006

SEPTEMBER	OCTOBER	NOVEMBER	DECEMBER
1 Fr	1 Su	1 We	1 Fr
2 Sa	**WEEK 40**	2 Th	2 Sa
3 Su	2 Mo	3 Fr	3 Su
WEEK 36	3 Tu	4 Sa	**WEEK 49**
4 Mo	4 We	5 Su ○	4 Mo
5 Tu	5 Th	**WEEK 45**	5 Tu ○
6 We	6 Fr	6 Mo	6 We
7 Th ○	7 Sa ○	7 Tu	7 Th
8 Fr	8 Su	8 We	8 Fr
9 Sa	**WEEK 41**	9 Th	9 Sa
10 Su	9 Mo	10 Fr	10 Su
WEEK 37	10 Tu	11 Sa	**WEEK 50**
11 Mo	11 We	12 Su ◐	11 Mo
12 Tu	12 Th	**WEEK 46**	12 Tu ◐
13 We	13 Fr	13 Mo	13 We
14 Th ◐	14 Sa ◐	14 Tu	14 Th
15 Fr	15 Su	15 We	15 Fr
16 Sa	**WEEK 42**	16 Th	16 Sa
17 Su	16 Mo	17 Fr	17 Su
WEEK 38	17 Tu	18 Sa	**WEEK 51**
18 Mo	18 We	19 Su	18 Mo
19 Tu	19 Th	**WEEK 47**	19 Tu
20 We	20 Fr	20 Mo ●	20 We ●
21 Th	21 Sa	21 Tu	21 Th
22 Fr ●	22 Su ●	22 We	22 Fr
23 Sa	**WEEK 43**	23 Th	23 Sa
24 Su	23 Mo	24 Fr	24 Su
WEEK 39	24 Tu	25 Sa	**WEEK 52**
25 Mo	25 We	26 Su	25 Mo
26 Tu	26 Th	**WEEK 48**	26 Tu
27 We	27 Fr	27 Mo	27 We ◑
28 Th	28 Sa	28 Tu ◑	28 Th
29 Fr	29 Su ◑	29 We	29 Fr
30 Sa ◑	**WEEK 44**	30 Th	30 Sa
	30 Mo		31 Su
	31 Tu		

ADDRESSES AND NOTES

ADDRESSES AND NOTES